How to
STAY FULL
of
THE HOLY SPIRIT

DR. DOYLE "BUDDY" HARRISON

FOREWORD

In the process of reprinting all of the classic books written by my late husband, Buddy Harrison, I have decided that the integrity of each book should be preserved, as is. All of his books were written by the inspiration of the Holy Spirit, and are still very relevant in the world we live in today. I believe God's Word is alive, and this book will give you great wisdom and insight, regardless of the date it was written. Some of the examples throughout his books may be a little dated, but they clearly show

Buddy's sense of humor and relevance in the particular time they were written. You may read some terms or colloquialisms that you aren't familiar with, that's okay, ask someone who is.

I trust this book will bless you.

Pat Harrison

HOW TO STAY FULL OF THE HOLY SPIRIT

This booklet is for those who have desired to move in the gifts of the Spirit but have never been able to, for those who have had difficulty entering into a freedom of praise and worship, and for those who have never been able to really get into intercession.

The open door to freedom in the Spirit is in Ephesians 5:15-21.

See then that ye walk circumspectly, not as fools, but as wise, redeeming the time, because the days are evil.

Wherefore be ye not unwise, but understanding what the will of the Lord is.

And be not drunk with wine, wherein is excess; but be filled with the Spirit; speaking to yourselves in psalms and hymns and spiritual songs, singing and making melody in your heart to the Lord; giving thanks always for all things unto God and the Father in the name of our Lord Jesus Christ; submitting yourselves one to another in the fear of God.

I would say that all Spirit-filled Christians want to walk in the wisdom of God. We all want to redeem time because of evil days, time that

Satan has stolen from us in one way or another. And we all want to understand the will of God for us. But few seem to know how to do any of this.

There have been a number of times in my life when I wanted and needed to know the will of God. I needed specific direction at a given moment, and I would look for Scripture verses that would speak to me and tell me what God's will was.

I remember once I was praying about going to a place in Minnesota as music and youth director. I prayed and searched the Scriptures to see if there was one that said, "Buddy Harrison, God said to go to Minnesota." I didn't find it, but I looked. I wanted one to say it just that plain because I wanted to walk in the wisdom of God.

Most of the time, we learn to walk by Biblical principles or through a witness to our spirit about whether to take a certain course or action. But the direction in these verses in Ephesians is written as much to each of us as if our names were listed there. The seven instructions are black and white, no shades of interpretations are necessary:

- Redeem the time. Understand the will of the Lord.

- Be filled with the Spirit, not drunk with wine. Speak to yourself in psalms, hymns and spiritual songs. Make melody in your heart to the Lord.

- Give thanks to God always for all things in the name of Jesus.

- Submit to one another in the fear of God.

Redeeming time depends on the fulfillment of the other six

instructions, and understanding the will of the Lord depends on being filled with the Spirit. How you can understand the will of the Lord after being filled is by speaking to yourself, singing and giving thanks to the Lord and submitting to one another.

What the Lord says in the third instruction is not to be drunk with the natural juice but to be so filled with the Holy Spirit that some of the characteristics of a drunkard show up in us. These things that are desirable when operating in the Spirit are perverted by Satan in an alcoholic.

A drunkard has no problems. He doesn't worry about tomorrow. He has no burdens and no cares. But it's an illusion. Tomorrow his cares will be back, multiplied. The Spirit-filled person who casts his cares on the Lord, however, truly can live carefree.

A drunkard will give you everything he has with total optimism that he can get more money or whatever he's giving without any trouble at all. The person "drunk" in the Spirit is free to give whatever the Lord tells him to, not out of a false optimism but in faith, knowing God is his source.

Christians who have never drunk of the Spirit of God are apt to keep themselves so rigid, so perfect, so exact that even when it comes time to praise God, they will look around to see who's watching and are unable to praise freely.

I'm not a Greek scholar, but I have been told by those who are that the tense of this verb, "be filled" with the Spirit, would better be translated by the phrase, "be constantly in the process of being filled."

Now the first evidence of being filled with the Spirit is your faith, and the first outward evidence is speaking in tongues as in the initial outpouring of the Holy Spirit on the Day of Pentecost. Being filled with the Spirit and then never speaking in tongues after the initial evidence is like taking a drink and then thinking you never need water again. It won't be an hour until you're thirsty.

Just because you had one drink does not mean you'll never need water again. It's not enough to take one drink of the Holy Spirit. You have to keep on drinking. It's a daily process to satisfy the thirst of your spirit, to sustain the spirit and enable you to grow.

Getting the Holy Spirit is not like a smallpox shot. If you don't use your prayer language, you lose the awareness of the Holy Spirit; you lose the consciousness of Him, and you lose the power that comes with operating in the Spirit.

All through the Book of Acts, it mentions the apostles being "filled with the Spirit." That does not mean they kept getting the initial evidence over and over, but that they constantly kept drinking and the infilling was an on-going process. (Acts 2,4,13.)

Now how did they do that? The next three verses — Ephesians 5:19-21 — tell how.

The fullness of the Spirit of God can be maintained by singing, giving thanks and submitting. The order of these is very important, and not an accident. Exhorting or speaking to yourself is a Bible pattern. David did it. The Bible says he encouraged himself in the Lord.

If you don't encourage yourself, many times there is no one else around to do it. Speak to yourself in other tongues and that will give you the capacity to sing a new song — the next step. God is the author of the new song. As a testimony in the mouths of two or three witnesses, look up these Scripture references:

Psalm 40:3, Psalm 96:1, Psalm 98:1, Psalm 144:9, Psalm 149:1, Isaiah 42:10, and Rev. 5:8,9.

The word "new" in the Greek means fresh. What God wants us to do is feed on His Spirit on a fresh basis. He wants us to have the fresh, not the old and stale. The scripture songs we sing today are fresh. They are not saying anything that has not been said before — the Bible says there is *nothing* new under the sun — but they are fresh.

What we sing on the spur of the moment by the Spirit of God is fresh because it is what the Spirit is prompting us to declare at that instant. In the first part of that 19th verse of Ephesians 5, you are speaking to yourself. Then you begin to speak to God.

There are songs written not to bless us but to worship and praise the Lord and Savior. Sometimes, you may start out by speaking to yourself and sing yourself right into victory, singing and making melody unto the Lord.

We must use this pattern to stay in a place of victory rather than despair. It is our obligation to activate and implement it. We can do it because the Holy Spirit has been given to us. He hasn't come on a two-week vacation. He is here to stay. You've got Him every day, so just start letting Him fill you every day.

There's no reason for you to have "blue Mondays." There's no reason to ever be despondent or whipped or down. There's no reason to feel defeated. When you understand this Biblical pattern for victory, you can sing and shout every day of your life. The verse that says to sing and make melody in your heart to the Lord falls into a different category.

Most people don't understand this part. I was confused for a number of years because of a misconception about God. The way I was brought up and taught caused me to think that all God wanted was workers. I really thought that was all He was interested in.

I didn't want to answer the call of God because I just knew He was going to send me to Africa as a missionary. I hadn't lost anything over there, and I wasn't looking for anything over there.

Now, I understand better what God wants. And I have been to Africa several times and plan to go again.

I thought God was looking for someone to do His dirty work, someone to get in there and do all the work. Someone to "go for it."

But God is not looking for workers. Let me show you the real heartbeat of God. It's in John 4:23.

But the hour cometh, and now

is, when the true worshippers shall worship the Father in spirit and in truth: for the Father seeketh such to worship him.

God is looking for worshipers, not workers. If He can find somebody who will worship Him, that person will come to a place of freedom, victory, and liberty, because worship will bring him into His presence. In the presence of the Lord is fullness of joy. When you get full of the joy of God, then you have the strength to do whatever He wants you to.

A Christian is not even a fit worker until he learns how to

worship. He is not capable of doing a work for the Lord until he first learns how to worship Him. Without worship, you are limited because, somewhere along the way, fear will overtake you. You will not be able to do what God wants you to do because you have not entered into His presence; you have not been the worshiper God wants.

The Holy Spirit is here to make us worshipers, but we have to avail ourselves of His help. We have to keep on speaking in other tongues, not just on the occasion of the initial filling but every day. Every day, we need to stir up the gifts and stay full. You can tell something is full when it runs over. You can tell somebody is getting full when tongues just comes bubbling out of their mouth.

If you don't ever hear from God, it is because you never minister to Him. The difference between believers today and many of those in days gone by is that believers today are willing to accept the responsibilities placed on them.

In years gone by, if they didn't understand events or the lack of power in Christian lives, they blamed somebody else or blamed God. If they didn't understand anything, it was "God's sovereign will." Today, we are starting to accept responsibility; we are starting to judge ourselves so that victory can come into our lives.

Now it is time for us to judge ourselves in the area of worship. God is seeking worshipers, and if we worship Him, then He will speak to us. If He is not speaking, then we are not worshiping. We are not ministering to Him, and that's the bottom line.

What David understood in his day, we have not understood in ours. In the tabernacle, there was worship 24 hours a day. We haven't understood that God wants His people worshiping Him all the time. The Church is worldwide so when some are asleep, others are awake.

In Psalm 134, those worshipers on the "night shift," those "servants of the Lord which stand by night," got tired and sleepy and started slacking up on the job. And they were told to start lifting up their hands. They weren't really praising God, just going through the motions and, consequently, they got tired and sleepy.

That is what happens in the Church much of the time. People

let down on their job; they let down their hands. Worship is any act or position taken which denotes the relative position of God and man. If God is above and we let our hands hang down, we're worshiping him who is beneath our feet.

A believer is supposed to walk with his head up, his shoulders back, his hands raised, saying, "Blessed is the Lamb of God Who taketh away the sins of the world."

After this I will return, and will build again the tabernacle of David, which is fallen down; and I will build again the ruins thereof, and I will set it up.

Acts 15:16

What tabernacle was that? The tabernacle of praise. That is what God is restoring to the earth today.

That is why people are singing, clapping their hands, shouting, dancing, running, jumping...praising the Lord every way possible. The sooner we line up with this and start praising God all day long, no matter what is happening or where we are, the more blessings are going to come into our lives.

Loud praise drives the devil nuts. It sends him out of his gourd! Loudness also is related to authority. The devil will not pay any attention to a sweet, passive person. The only thing he understands is force, supernatural force. That force is the Holy Spirit.

You don't play games with the devil. There is a direct correlation between the loud cry and the voice of authority. A passive individual will be run over all his life. The Bible tells us that we are an army. An army is not a passive group. When we make up our minds to go ahead and possess the land, that means we are going to have to fight for it.

When you feel empty or barren, or when you are in trouble, learn to reach down on the inside of you and let the power of God come out.

He that believeth on me, as the scripture hath said, out of his belly shall flow rivers of living water.

John 7:38

When the devil is attacking you or your family, when you are dealing with the forces of hell, you need that power like a river, not like a stream or a trickle of water.

When you break forth into crying aloud and singing to God, you break spiritual barrenness. Then growth will come. Enlargement will come, both for the church that praises and worships and for the individual.

> **Sing, O barren, thou that didst not bear; break forth into singing, and cry aloud, thou that didst not travail with child: for more are the children of the desolate than the children of the married wife, saith the Lord.**
>
> **Enlarge the place of thy tent, and let them stretch forth the curtains of thine habitations...**
>
> **For thou shalt break forth on the right hand and on the left.**
>
> Isaiah 54:1-3

Start "breaking forth" the singing on a regular basis and you will have to enlarge the place. When your captivity gets turned when the time is redeemed — you'll be singing. A church that doesn't sing, doesn't really worship God. Music is a vital part of worship and praise. Speaking to yourself and singing to the Lord are to be done in "all things," as well as giving thanks.

Not just in good times or when you are happy, but in bad times or in the midst of persecution. The same pattern will bring victory and the working out of God's will.

Remember in Acts, chapter 16, Paul and Silas were in jail, persecuted for preaching the Gospel. What did they do? They sang praises unto God. And they didn't sing quietly or passively, because the Bible says very clearly, "and the prisoners heard them."

There is a good possibility that their backs were beaten, but they were singing loudly enough for the praises to be heard down the corridors of that prison. Freedom came through their singing. An earthquake loosened their bonds, and they were able, in addition, to lead an entire household to Christ.

Freedom will come to you when you begin to sing and minister unto the Lord.

Most people can't see the good in situations that seem bad in the natural. But Paul did. He took the opportunity of being in prison in later years to write most of his epistles. And where would the Body of Christ have been down through the centuries without Paul's letters? Most people can't see the positive side of bad situations. They can't see how God can take that situation and bless it and turn it around.

Whom the Son has set free is free indeed. Jail doesn't mean anything. It doesn't matter what comes. We are free in God. When we start singing and giving thanks unto God in all things, it becomes easier to submit to one another.

Husbands and wives live in conflict sometimes. Wives want to submit, but don't know how. Speaking to themselves and singing unto the Lord will break that bondage of self and enable them to walk in love.

Many church members can't submit to the pastor, and I'll tell you why. They don't minister to the

Lord, they don't speak to themselves, they don't give thanks in all things, therefore they stay in a rebellious, self-centered attitude.

Practicing the instructions in these verses from Ephesians, even when you don't feel like it, will also open up the operation of the gifts of the Spirit to you. The Holy Spirit will have freedom to manifest in His various aspects, or characteristics, through your life. Start ministering to the Lord in private, in your personal devotions. Don't expect God to use you in public when you can't do it privately.

The Bible says, **Prove all things; hold fast that which is good** (1 Thess. 5:21). If you have not proven the voice of God in your private times with Him, you won't be sure it's His voice when the time comes for public demonstration. Start praying or singing in tongues, then pray with the "understanding," as Paul said.

Your spirit gets built up by speaking in tongues, but your mind doesn't get anything out of it. For the mind to get built up spiritually, you need the interpretation of what has been said in tongues. The way to begin operating in interpretation is to pray in tongues until you sense a satisfaction in the spirit, then stop and begin listening for words in English.

Start speaking out those words. If it doesn't sound right in the beginning, keep on going. The more you do it, the more sure you will become. Your mind will be refreshed because it will know what the Spirit is saying. Oral Roberts built a multi-million-dollar facility that is blessing thousands upon thousands of lives today because he understood this principle.

Everything about the City of Faith — its design, the entire building, the principles by which it operates, the people who are there and their job responsibilities — came to Brother Roberts through his speaking in tongues and then interpreting in English what the Holy Spirit was saying.

His Holy Spirit is the same as yours. You can do the same thing, if you are in the process of being constantly filled. You can pray out the answers about your business, any marriage difficulties, problems with your children, or any other problems. You can turn around and get directions from headquarters: wisdom, answers that are not just mental and half-heard, but clear directions.

If you'll enter into praise and worship and begin with that, you will be able to get into that other dimension where you can pray some things out and not have to wander around questioning everybody else: *Is this God's will for me?* You'll know what God's will is, and you'll know the voice of God.

Most of us want to do as Peter did in the walking-on-water incident. He wanted to prove it was the voice of the Master. Isn't that what most of us want to do at times? We want to prove that it is the voice of God speaking to us. Some people seem to think that asking God to repeat something is unbelief.

But there's nothing wrong with proving all things and holding fast to that which is good.

If I didn't hear the Lord clearly, I want to hear the instruction again. I've been moving in the gifts under the Holy Spirit on a public platform and didn't hear something He said to me. I'd have to stop and say, "Say that again, Lord."

Do you think God struck me dead on the spot? No, He understands. His nature is to reassure us. So if you didn't get something straight that you believe He said to you, then keep asking, and He will say it again. Then you learn to prove what is the voice of God so that when an utterance comes to you in church, you won't be wondering, "Should I give this, or not?"

God wants you to know that you know that you know. He is not a hit-or-miss, could-be, might-be, maybe-so, hope-so God. He is an absolute. He is known as "the Great

I Am." He doesn't offer us uncertainties. He offers us surety, absoluteness, guarantees. When you start seeing Him in that light, you will be sure of yourself.

Other people may think it is cockiness, being that sure of the voice of God. But you *can* be sure of His voice. Then you will be able to operate decently and in order, in submission to the way your church operates in the ministry of the gifts.

The Holy Spirit is God's gift to the Church and the ministries of the gifts of the Spirit are the ways in which He manifests in and to the

Body. God is not going to ask us to do a task and not give us the equipment to do it. Jesus told us in Luke 19:13 to "occupy" until He returns, and "occupying" means spreading the good news of salvation, healing the sick, casting out demons, and even raising the dead.

The power or the "tools," with which to do these things comes from the Holy Spirit. And that's where a whole lot of Christians are in trouble. They are trying to do these things without the Holy Spirit. They are digging ditches without shovels.

If you stay continually filled with the Spirit, then you can reach down inside your own spirit and pull out the power.

Start by speaking in tongues. Proceed with the interpretation, then sing in tongues and praise the Lord. After that, you can move up a level and speak or sing by prophecy.

Do you see the order of this? It takes more faith to prophesy. You don't ever get to the gifts that require more faith and power until you are faithful in the lower-level ones. A pastor can't have a congregation of thousands until he is faithful with the few he has in the beginning. That's a principle.

Before you get out of bed in the morning, you ought to sing and pray in tongues. In fact, it wouldn't hurt to go to sleep praying in tongues. This is one of the most realistic, practical ways of moving into the supernatural realm that I know.

If you cannot take the Word of God and apply it in everyday life, then something is wrong. Theology without a practical application is not worth two bits. God intends for us to use all of His Word. He gave us the Holy Spirit, the Comforter, for a purpose.

If you don't encourage yourself in the Lord, He's not going to comfort you. You're not a baby anymore and He expects you to learn to walk. Begin by encouraging yourself in the Lord. Talk to yourself. Those moments when you're hurt, when somebody has said something nasty or hurtful, are the times to pray in tongues.

If you follow Ephesians 5:18-21, you will move into operating in the gifts of the Spirit; you will move into intercession, and you can shake off all the burdens that have attached themselves to you. You will also have freedom in praise and worship — and fewer problems with submitting to other people.

There are times when I get so busy with running all the things I'm involved in that it seems I can't stand any more details. I just turn around and walk out of the office and go home. I walk through the house singing in tongues, singing the interpretation, praising God. I get myself built up again, charged up and ready to go.

I couldn't face the problems I have to face without this. You don't deal with hundreds of churches, a publishing company, thousands of ministers, and many Bible schools without facing some problems. There has to be somewhere to go for answers, somewhere to go for comfort, and some way to get the mind of God on how to solve problems and how to do some things.

My wife Pat and I have been married over 25 years, and one of the reasons our marriage survived in the early years is that we would take one another in our arms and pray in tongues together. Through this God built a bond and a dynamic love between us.

When the storms of life came, when a young man's stupidity and ignorance tried to overtake me, I had learned to give place to the Holy Spirit, and He was able to see me through hard times and stupid mistakes. The first seven years were like hell on earth, and I created most of it through immaturity and stupidity. But the Spirit of God kept working with me and worked all these things out in my life.

So I know by personal experience that the Holy Spirit can change your life, turn it around and resolve any problem. The key is to remain continually filled through speaking to yourself, singing a new song in praise and worship, and thanking God in all things.

Dr. Doyle (Buddy) Harrison
(1939-1998)

Buddy Harrison lived his life full of the love of God, with a vision for the supernatural church.

Buddy was raised in Houston, Texas, and, as a boy, was healed of paralyzing polio. At the age of 19, he married Pat Hagin. In 1964, Buddy and Pat stepped out into full-time ministry, as youth and choir directors in Minneapolis, Minnesota, before moving to

Tulsa, Oklahoma, to serve for 10 years as administrators for Kenneth Hagin Ministries. In November 1975, Buddy and Pat Harrison launched Harrison House Publishers, releasing their first titles in 1976. Since then, Harrison House has been a vehicle for ministers to get their messages in print, and has published and distributed more than 100 million books in 42 languages and in more than 175 countries.

In November 1977, the Lord spoke to Co-Founders Buddy and Pat Harrison, "Go back to Tulsa, start a family church, a Bible teaching center, and reach the world." And so began Faith Christian Fellowship International, as a local church in Tulsa, OK, in January 1978.

The church grew rapidly; and, by the end of its second year, was averaging more than 1,900 members. FCF of Tulsa was one of the first Word of Faith churches in the area. During this time, the Word of Faith movement exploded through men and women of God in Tulsa.

The Lord used the Harrisons to start a great revival of God's Word and the supernatural ministry of the Holy Spirit. From FCF of Tulsa, men and women looked to the Harrisons for leadership, as they went throughout the nation and around the world, starting churches and Bible schools.

In 1981, while the Harrisons were in Jerusalem with Dr. Lester Sumrall, the Lord told them that they were a "Pastor to pastors and ministers." This led Buddy and Pat to begin the International Office that, to this day, helps hundreds of churches and thousands of ministers worldwide. FCF has resident ministry in 53 nations. In addition to churches around the world, FCF family members also have Bible schools, orphanages, and various humanitarian outreaches.

When Buddy Harrison went home to be with the Lord on November 28, 1998, Pat Harrison assumed full responsibility for leading the FCF family. Men and women, who have many years of ministerial experience, assist her in fulfilling the vision and mission of FCF. The vision of Faith Christian Fellowship

International is "Helping You Fulfill the Vision and Call God Has Given."

To this day, the legacy of Buddy and Pat Harrison continues, as their daughter, Cookie Brothers, who is now CEO of FCF International, leads the organization, which *Connects* relationally with leaders and ministries, equipping them to *Achieve* the vision God has given, and empowering them to walk in their Divine *Destiny.*